Wook Books

COZY CHRISTMAS

PRO TIP!

When using wet mediums such as markers, place a blank sheet of paper behind the coloring page to prevent bleed-through.

THANK YOU FOR YOUR PURCHASE!

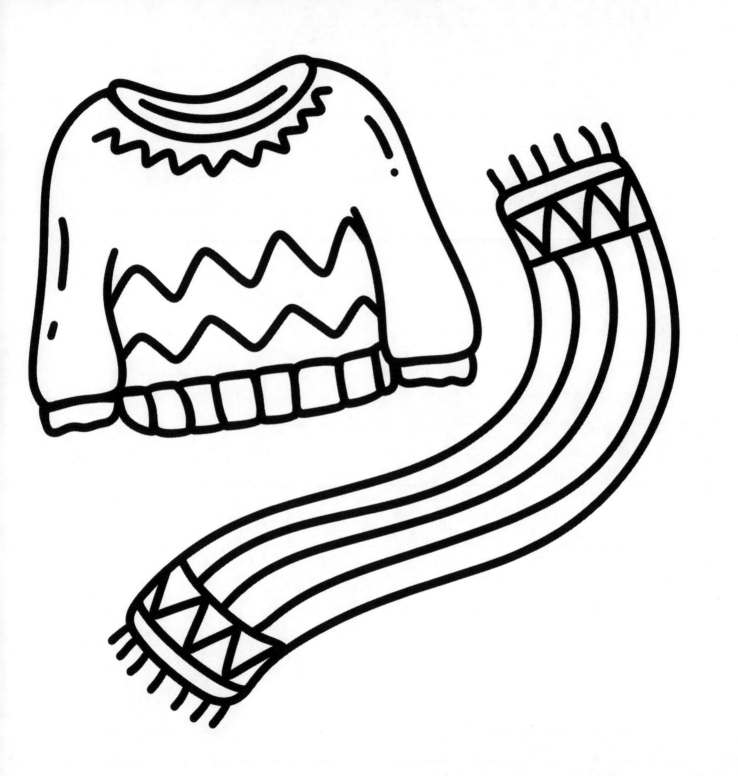

Made in the USA
Columbia, SC
18 February 2025

54061793R00048